by Melvin Jefferson
illustrated by Julia Gorton

BOSTON

Printed in China

ISBN 10: 0-618-88667-2
ISBN 13: 978-0-618-88667-8

10 11 12 0940 17 16 15 14
4500466953

My brother and I play a game with shape pieces. We like to see who can make a picture using the most pieces.

 How many pieces do you see?

I take 4 pieces. What can I make?

I know, I'll make a boat.

10 – 4 How many pieces are left?

I put my pieces back.
It's my brother's turn.

4 + 6 How many pieces are there in all?

My brother takes 6 pieces.

He makes a tall tower.

10 – 6 How many pieces are left now?

My brother puts his pieces back.
I take 4 pieces and make a castle.

 10 – 4 How many pieces are left?

My brother takes 6 pieces and adds them on to mine. We make a rocket ship using all the pieces.

4 + 6 How many pieces did they use?

Blast Off!

Draw

Look at page 7. Draw the rocket ship you see.

Tell About

Draw Conclusions Look at page 7. Tell about the different shapes that make up the rocket ship.

Write

Look at page 7. Write the number of shapes the children used to make the rocket ship.